Journey to Success

"See the Vision...Create Your Path"

Erica M. Odom

Owner of Odom Investments & Property Management LLC

WestBow Press books may be ordered through booksellers or by contacting:

WestBow Press
A Division of Thomas Nelson & Zondervan
1663 Liberty Drive
Bloomington, IN 47403
www.westbowpress.com
844-714-3454

Because of the dynamic nature of the Internet, any web addresses or links contained in this book may have changed since publication and may no longer be valid. The views expressed in this work are solely those of the author and do not necessarily reflect the views of the publisher, and the publisher hereby disclaims any responsibility for them.

Any people depicted in stock imagery provided by Getty Images are models, and such images are being used for illustrative purposes only.
Certain stock imagery © Getty Images.

ISBN: 978-1-6642-7616-1 (sc)
ISBN: 978-1-6642-7617-8 (e)

Library of Congress Control Number: 2022915581

Print information available on the last page.

WestBow Press rev. date: 10/27/2022

WESTBOW
PRESS®
A DIVISION OF THOMAS NELSON
& ZONDERVAN

Introduction

Success is when you are happy with your results, not when someone else is. Are you looking to own a home? Tired of renting or living with your parents? Do you think you are ready for that next step? Maybe you are. Maybe you need to be more informed on the process. Perhaps, you just need someone there to help you decide what comes next. My focus is more on where you want to be than where you are or where you have come from. No one has ever won a race starting at the finish line. Home ownership is much the same. You must start at the beginning and have the passion and motivation to see it through to the end. You will hear me speak about the journey, and rightfully so. I believe in the process, and I know the process is a journey. I don't have a magic potion or a quick 1, 2, 3 scheme to get you there overnight. However, what I do have are tried and tested methods, reliable knowledge, and sound guidance. So, if you are ready to roll up your sleeves and get on the road, I am excited to have you on board and look forward to showing you what's possible.

Meet Your Author

My name is Erica Odom, and I am the founder of Odom Investments & Property Management LLC. I am an advanced practice licensed social worker, with a master's degree in social work. I also have an associate degree in criminal justice. I am a college instructor, a landlord, a real estate investor, a licensed life agent, a success coach, and a project manager. Here is my story. In 2006, I purchased my first property, a duplex home for $125,000. This was before the recessed economy and the memorable housing market crash of 2008. So many people lost not only their livelihood, but also defaulted on their mortgage loans and lost their homes and security. I was an inexperienced 19-year-old young adult with a decent credit score and a consistent employment history. My mortgage broker approved me for a loan, and I purchased my duplex. My loan was an 80/20 loan, which consisted of 80% of the loan being an ARM (Adjustable-Rate Mortgage), and 20% of the loan being a balloon payment. I rented out half of my duplex and lived in the other half for about five years. Throughout those years, I watched my property depreciate. In addition, my adjustable ARM loan was scheduled to adjust within a year. I reached out to my mortgage company for help but was told there was nothing they could do because my mortgage loan was current, and I would need to be in default on the loan to get assistance. I could not get a bank to approve me for the refinancing of my loans, because my debt-to-income ratio was high. I made the decision to stop making my mortgage payments. I decided I was not going to put another dime towards this property. I didn't quite know what I was going to do, however, I knew I had to do something and quickly. I also made the decision to put the house up for sale as a short sale, in April of 2013. It sold for $15,000 cash to an investor. In December of 2017, I was able to rebuild my credit and build up my savings from the loss I had taken in 2013, and today continue to grow in my real estate journey. In December of 2018, I founded my company in Milwaukee, WI.

Contents

Preparing for The Journey

(Module 1)

What Is Your Why?

_____
_____
_____
_____
_____
_____
_____
_____
_____

What Is Your Goal?

Let's break this down:

Specific: What do you want to accomplish? Who is involved? What city are you looking to purchase a home?

Measurable: How much? How many?

Attainable: Is your goal realistic based on your current financial factors?

Realistic: Is this the right time for you to purchase a home?

Time-bound: When are you looking to purchase a home by?

Example:

General Goal: I want to buy a home.

SMART Goal: My husband and I want to buy a single-family home in Milwaukee, WI for a purchase price less than $150,000, within 2 years from today's date.

Now you write it out.

Specific: _____
_____
_____

Measurable: _____
_____
_____

Attainable: _____
_____
_____

Realistic: _____
_____
_____

Time-bound: _____
_____
_____

My Goal: _____
_____
_____

What's Your Vision?

Questions to Consider

1. What is your total debt today? What are your plans to eliminate the debt you owe? Do you have an emergency fund? Do you have extra money saved? How do you plan to save or get extra income?

2. What are you looking for in a property? (i.e., single family, condo, multi-family)

3. Are you looking to become a homeowner, landlord, or investor?

Where Are You Today?

Notes: _____
_____
_____
_____
_____
_____
_____

Who Are You?

What's the difference between the rich and poor?

Mindset...

Poor

Focused on looking rich

Waiting on someone to come and save them

Buys beyond their means

Uses credit because they don't have cash

Carries a balance on credit cards

Doesn't have money management skills

Rich

Focused on being rich

Buys luxury after they hit their money goal

Buys within their means

Set financial goals

Teaches themselves financial literacy

Relies on only themselves

Are you living rich or poor?

_____

_____

_____

_____

_____

What can you change?

_____

_____

_____

_____

_____

On a scale from 0-10, 0 being not ready at all and 10 being extremely ready, how ready are you to change your financial Journey?

| 0 | 1 | 2 | 3 | 4 | 5 | 6 | 7 | 8 | 9 | 10 |

FOUR USES OF CASH

U Unexpected Expenses and Emergencies
  - Job Loss, Unplanned Medical Bill, Home Repair, Auto Repair

S Specific Short-term Savings Goals
  - Vacation, Wedding, New Car

E Everyday Spending
  - Groceries, Utilities, Rent, Entertainment, Insurance, Gas, Other Debts

S Sources of Investment
  - Real Estate, Stocks, Bonds, Cash

What area of use are you putting most of your cash? (Circle One)

A.) Unexpected Expenses and Emergencies
B.) Specific Short-term Savings Goals
C.) Everyday Spending
D.) Sources of Investment

Budget and Savings

Smart Strategies

- Smart Spending
- Debt Consolidation
- Payoff Strategies (Snowball Method)
- Emergency Fund ($1,000 minimum)
- Have a Checking and Savings Account
- Know Uses of Cash
- Catch Up on Past Due Accounts
- Monitor Your Credit

Resources:

- How the Debt Snowball Method Works | RamseySolutions.com
- https://www.ramseysolutions.com/dave-ramsey-7-baby-steps

Your Budgeting Tool Kit:

- o Budget Cash Envelopes
- o Budgeting Tracker Sheet
- o Snowball Method

Success Check-in:

1. What has been your budgeting and savings successes?
2. What are your challenges currently?

Notes: _____

_____

_____

_____

_____

_____

_____

Retirement Accounts

Types of Account:

- • 401K
- • 403B
- • Traditional IRA (Individual Retirement Account)
- • Roth IRA

Benefits When Buying a Home

o Can possibly use money for your down payment
o Some plans will allow you to use funds for real estate investment options
o **Loan** against your money for your down payment and avoid tax penalties
o Account is considered an **asset**
o Internal Revenue Service (IRS) defines a **first-time homebuyer** as any person who has not lived in a home they've owned in the last **2 years**, even if they owned a home previously. If married, your spouse must meet the same requirements to qualify.
o IRA: Can withdraw up to $10,000 over a lifetime for first-time home buyer purchases. You will not be subject to a tax penalty, but it is subject to income taxes.
o Roth IRA: If you've owned an account for at least **5 year**s; any distributions used for a first-time home purchase is considered a qualified distribution, which means you will be exempt from paying income tax and a penalty. If you've owned the account less than five years, you may avoid penalties, but may be subject to income tax.

Credit Basics 101

Credit Score:
Range: 300–850
Best Rates: **740+**

Credit Bureaus:

Equifax:
https://www.equifax.com/personal/
1 (888) 548-7878

Experian:
https://www.experian.com/
1 (888) 397-3742

TransUnion:
https://www.transunion.com/
1 (800) 916-8800

Credit Resources:

- www.myFICO.com
- www.AnnualCreditReport.com
- www.consumer.ftc.gov

Credit Score Factors

- History of on-time payments
- Credit utilization
- Length of credit history
- Recent searches for credit (Inquiries)
- Types of credit used

What Is Affecting Your Credit Score?

- ☐ **Payment History**-Late Payments (i.e., 30 days late)
- ☐ **Negative Information** (i.e., Public Records, late accounts, collections, foreclosures, repossessions)
  Note: Negative items and chapter 13 bankruptcy can stay on the report for up to 7 years and chapter 7 bankruptcy for up to 10 years
- ☐ Not paying medical bills
- ☐ Student Loans
- ☐ Too many **HARD inquires**
- ☐ **Credit Utilization** (i.e., Balances over 30%)
- ☐ **Credit Length** (No credit history)
- ☐ **Credit Mix** (Not enough variety in accounts)

Now let's look at your credit: www.AnnualCreditReport.com
Action Steps:

_____
_____
_____
_____
_____
_____

Ways to Improve Your Credit

- Pay your bills on time (before 30th day)
- Pay student loans and medical bills on time
- Stop applying for credit (soft inquiries are okay)
- Keep credit card balances below 30%
  (i.e., if your credit limit is $300, you should always have $210 available in credit)
- Have a good credit mix (i.e., auto loan, credit card)
- Pay down revolving accounts
- Open a secured credit card
- Become an authorized user
- Minimize your debt
- Monitor your credit regularly
- Practice responsible spending habits

Success Check-in:

What action steps have you completed?

What action steps still need to be completed?

What has been challenging for you to achieve?

What has been working well for you?

Notes: _____

_____

_____

_____

_____

_____

_____

_____

_____

_____

_____

_____

_____

_____

Credit Cards

Credit Cards and Minimum Payments Source:

New Balance	$1,786.00
Minimum Payment Due	$53.00
Payment Due Date	2/13/20

Late Payment Warning: If we do not receive your minimum payment by the date listed above, you may have to pay a $35 fee and your APRs may be increased up to the penalty rate of 28.99%.

Minimum Payment Warning: If you make only the minimum payment each period, you will pay more in interest, and it will take you longer to pay off your balance.

If you make no additional charges using this card and each month you pay ...	You will pay off the balance shown on this statement in about ...	And you will end up paying an estimated total of ...
Only the minimum payment	8 years	$2,785
$62	3 years	$2,232 (Savings = $553)

Case Examples

Review the case examples below. Circle the correct answer.

Case Example #1

Linda has a $1000 Macy's credit card limit. How much of her credit limit should Linda spend?

A. $0   N/A
B. $950   95% utilization
C. $250   25% utilization

Case Example # 2

Derek is looking to build his credit. He went to his bank and was approved for a visa credit card. His credit limit is $300. He decided he would use $75 of his available credit limit in the month of May for gas. When should he pay the card balance off?

A. Pay his balance off by his next due date
B. Take 2-3 months to pay off his card
C. Pay the minimum balance

"A winner is a dreamer who never gives up"
-Nelson Mandela

Other Things to Consider

Whole Life Insurance Policy vs Termed Life Insurance Policy

Whole Life Insurance Policy: Whole life insurance also known as a permanent policy, is a policy that is more expensive, and it builds cash value over time. Unlike a term policy, whole life remains active for the entire life of the policyholder, if premiums have been paid. The beneficiaries will receive a set death benefit upon the insured's death.

Cash Value Benefits:

- A living benefit that works as a savings account the insured can access throughout their lifetime
- Policy loan can be taken and paid back on a flexible repayment plan with low interest rates
- The premium payments earn interest and builds cash value on a tax-free basis

VS

Termed Life Policy: The termed life policy pays out a set death benefit upon the insured's death. These polices are more affordable and are not lifelong polices. These policies expire within 10, 15, 20, 30, or 35 years automatically.

What Is Generational Wealth?

Generational wealth includes financial assets such as property, investments, money, or anything with a monetary value that you pass down from one generation to the next. Keep in mind, it is important that you are passing along financial education and good habits to family members during the process.

How To Build Generational Wealth

1. Invest in your child's education
2. Invest in the stock market
3. Invest in real estate
4. Create a business to pass down
5. Take advantage of life insurance

How To Pass Generational Wealth

1. **Write a Will:** This provides specific instructions on your last wishes and assets. A will maps out what you want done with your financial assets, and who will be appointed the guardian for your minor

children. When you don't have a will, the state will determine who will become the guardian of your children and makes the decision on what happens to your property and assets.

2. **Set Up a Trust:** A trust, also known as a trust fund, is a legal entity that you can hold your assets in and have transferred to your beneficiaries. A trust fund is also a safe option you can use to ensure that your children receive your assets through payments or a lump sum payment. A child can access the trust fund between ages 18-21.

3. **Name Account Beneficiaries:** To ensure that your assets pass down to the beneficiaries of your choice, it is important to list a specific beneficiary on all your accounts, including your savings and checking accounts.

The Pre-Approval Process

(Module 2)

How to Find the Right Lender

Here are some questions to consider asking:

- What is the cost for the appraisal fee?
- Is there an application fee or any hidden fees?
- What is the required <u>minimum</u> credit score?
- What is the DTI (debt-to-income ratio) requirement?
- How many months of reserves do I need saved?
- How quickly can we close on the loan? *(i.e., 30 or 45 days?)*
- Do you offer any incentives towards closing cost, or first-time home buyer grants?
- Will you sell my loan to another lender after I close on my home?
- What loan products do you carry? *(i.e., VA, FHA, Conventional)*
- Do you offer a rate lock?
- Do you charge prepayment penalties on your loans?
- What is required for down payment? *(i.e., 3%, 5%, 10%, or 20% down)*
- Do you have any down payment assistance programs?
- What does the preapproval and closing process look like?

Action Steps:

Contact (3) lenders of your choice.

1. _____
2. _____
3. _____

Success Check-in: What did you discover during your search? Which lender best suits your lending needs?

Notes: _____
_____
_____
_____
_____
_____
_____

Coffee Date with Realtor

Finding the BEST realtor for you is essential to your journey. Below are some questions to consider when selecting a realtor.

- **How long have you been a realtor?**
- **Tell me about your experience**
- **Are you a full-time or part-time realtor?**
- **What is your flexibility for scheduling showings?**
- **What other advertising sources do you utilize for listing a home besides MLS** (Multiple Listings Service)?
- **How much is your commission when I buy or sale a home?**

Action Steps: Have a coffee date with at least (3) realtors of your choice.

1. _____
2. _____
3. _____

Success Check-in: What has your experience been like up until this point while searching for a lender and a realtor? What is working well? What is not working well? Have you chosen a lender or realtor to work with?

Notes: _____
_____
_____
_____
_____
_____
_____
_____

Home Inspector Must Knows...

Home Inspections can be costly but are worth the cost. The buyer and inspector will meet to walk through the home. It is important that the buyer uses the inspection as an opportunity to ask questions and be educated about the home. The inspection points out imperfections in a home, at which point the buyer can also potentially use some of the findings to negotiate by requesting that the seller fix things, and request additional inspections (i.e., mold inspector, structural engineer), and or a buyer's credit. This is an upfront cost for the buyer.

Key things to pay close attention to when completing a home inspection are:
Foundation, Roof, Plumbing, Electrical Systems, HVAC System, Mold

<u>Questions to Consider When Looking for the Best Home Inspector</u>

- **Are they licensed and insured** (State of Wisconsin requires license)
- **How long are their home inspections** (Most typically run 2-3 hours)
- **How detailed is the inspection report** (Ask to see a sample report)
- **Do they educate during the inspection or just quickly walk through**
- **What do others say** (Recommendations)

Action Steps: Find (3) local home inspectors.

List below the home inspectors you have spoken with.

1. _____
2. _____
3. _____

Rodent Infestation   Foundation Cracks/Bowing   Mold

Homeowner's Insurance

Homeowners insurance policies generally cover destruction and damage to a buyer's property. The policy covers damage to the interior and exterior of the property, covers loss from a theft of possessions, and covers personal liability for harm to others.

It is recommended that buyers check with their insurance company that holds their auto policy, as often time discounts can be applied for having multiple policies. Buyers will need to be prepared to pay the first-year premium cost for their insurance at closing. This cost is typically included in the closing cost expenses.

The Pre-Approval Process

Pre-qualification: This is simply just an estimate of how much someone can afford to spend on a home.

Pre-approval: This is more valuable than a pre-qualification and often required when submitting an offer to purchase. The lender has looked at the potential buyer's credit and verified the documentation to approve a specific loan amount. This pre-approval is valid **60-90 days**. After this timeframe, the potential buyer will need to get pre-approved again.

Needed Documents

- ❑ Verify Income (i.e., recent paystub)
  Part-time Jobs: Income can only be used if you have been employed for at least **2 years**

- ❑ Verify Assets (i.e., bank statements, retirement account statements)
- ❑ Pull All Credit Reports (lender uses buyer's middle score)
- ❑ Other Documentation (i.e., driver's license, identification card, social security number)

Debt-To-Income Ratio (DTI)

This compares an individual's monthly debt payments to their monthly gross income.

Monthly Gross Income: Your income before taxes and other deductions are deducted.

Lenders typically will allow you to have a DTI of **41-45%**, but it depends on the lender. Try to stay at a DTI of *41%* or lower. **https://www.credit.com/calculators/dti/**

When You Find a Home

Step 1: Purchase Agreement
A legal document between the seller and buyer. The agreement describes the terms and conditions of the sale, to ensure that both parties will follow through on their promises regarding the sale.

Step 2: Earnest Money
A deposit made to the seller, that represents a buyer's good faith to buy a home. This deposit usually ranges $500-$1,000 and is submitted typically within **3 days** after signing the offer to purchase agreement.

Step 3: Notify Lender and Begin Loan Application Process

Step 4: Loan Estimate
Buyer receives this document within **3 days** of completing a loan application. The loan estimate outlines important details about the loan they have requested.

Home Search Engines

- Realtor.com
- Wihomes.com
- Zillow.com
- Milwaukee.gov (*City of Milwaukee Properties*)
- Have realtor send listings to your email (MLS)
- Hudhomes.com (*Housing & Urban Development*)

The Mortgage Loan Application Process

(Module 3)

The buyer is now at the phase of their homebuying process where they have secured a home and have an accepted offer to purchase agreement. Use the checklist below to gather your needed loan application documents.

Loan Application Checklist

	Application Fee (*if applicable*)
	Driver's license or identification card
	Social security number or ITIN number
	Residential addresses for the past two years
	Name and address of employer (s) for past two years
	W-2's for the past two years
	Copies of most recent tax returns
	If self-employed, profit and loss statements and tax returns for the past two years
	Additional income verification (*i.e., child support payments*)
	All bank account statements for the past two months
	List of assets and their value (*i.e., retirement funds, life insurance, stocks/bonds*)
	Letter of explanations (*i.e., negative items on credit, gaps in employment*)
	Chapter 7 or 13 discharge letter
	Divorce Decree
	If applying for VA loan; Certificate of Eligibility

What to Expect During the Loan Processing Phase

Step 1-Submit Documentation: Submit your offer to purchase agreement to your lender, including all documents from the checklist. Typically, realtors will submit the offer to purchase agreement for you. Remember to submit all forms when requested in a timely matter, as submitting not in a timely matter can cause your closing to become delayed.

Step 2-Underwriting: The buyer's lender has their file together and has all needed documents. The buyer's loan is submitted to make sure they meet the minimum requirements of a home loan. If the loan is rejected by the underwriter, it is kicked back to the mortgage broker or loan officer, to gather more required information from the buyer. The underwriting department sometimes will request the buyer to write a **Letter of Explanation**, which is a letter that explains negative items or incorrect items on buyer's credit report.

Online Homebuyer's Training Course: Some lenders require that you take their online homebuying course. The course may cost, and the price varies.

Homeowner's Insurance: Homeowners insurance policies generally cover destruction and damage to a buyer's property. The policy covers damage to the interior and exterior of the property, covers loss from a theft of possessions, and covers personal liability for harm to others.

It is recommended that buyers check with their insurance company that holds their auto policy, as often time discounts can be applied for having multiple policies. Buyers will need to be prepared to pay the first-year premium cost for their insurance at closing. This cost is typically included in the closing cost expenses.

The Final Stages

Escrow Account: This account is used to hold monthly payments towards property taxes, homeowner's insurance, and mortgage insurance. The first-year premium of homeowner's insurance and property taxes are calculated within the closing cost expenses.

Upfront Cost (Capital): This includes earnest money, inspection fee, appraisal fee, down payment, closing cost, and moving expenses.

Closing Cost: Closing costs are processing fees buyers pay to their lender when they close on their real estate transaction. Closing costs on a mortgage loan usually equals **3 – 6%** of the total loan amount. Closing costs may include fees related to the origination and underwriting of a mortgage loan, real estate commissions, taxes, and insurance premiums, as well as title and record filings. Buyer and sellers are subject to paying various closing cost expenses.

Mortgage Reserves (Your Liquid): These are cash assets and other assets that you can convert to cash. These assets are not used towards closing cost or down payment.

Examples of Liquid Reserves

- Checking and Savings Account
- Stock or Bonds Investments
- Certificate of Deposits (CD's)
- Trust Accounts
- 401K, IRA, Retirement Accounts
- Cash Value of a vested Life Insurance Policy

Adjustable-Rate Mortgage (ARM): This is a risky option, because after the initial period of the loan, the interest rate adjusts over time based on the market.

Fixed Interest Rate: Interest rate is the same throughout the life of the loan.

Balloon Payment: This is a short-term loan, that is typically used for mortgages on commercial loans. A portion of the loan principal balance is amortized (spread out) over the period of the loan. The remaining balance is due at the end of the loan. This will result in the buyer paying a large payment at the term of the balloon loan.

Private Mortgage Insurance: Private mortgage insurance, also called **PMI**, is a type of mortgage insurance the buyer may be required to pay for if they have a conventional loan. PMI protects the lender not the buyer, in the event the buyer defaults on their loan. PMI is usually required when buyers make a down payment of less than **20%** of the home's purchase price. If buyers are refinancing with a conventional loan and their equity is less than 20 percent of the value of their home, PMI is also usually required.

Mortgage Insurance Premium: Mortgage insurance premium, also called **MIP** is a type of insurance the buyer is required to pay for a federal housing administration loan (FHA). MIP protects the lender not the buyer, in the event the buyer defaults on the loan. Buyers will pay an upfront premium cost at closing. The annual MIP payment is typically added to the buyer's monthly mortgage payment.

Since June 3, 2013, buyers are eligible for MIP to be removed only if the buyer made a **10%** or greater down payment and has made on-time mortgage payments for the last **11 years**. Buyers who pay less than 10% down, will be required to pay MIP for the life of the loan. If buyers don't meet these requirements, they will need to refinance their FHA loan into a conventional loan.

Loan Contingencies

Home Inspection Contingency: Home Inspections can be costly but are worth the cost. The buyer and inspector will meet to walk through the home. It is important that buyer uses the inspection as an opportunity to ask questions and be educated about the home. The inspection points out imperfections in a home, at which point the buyer can also potentially use some of the findings to negotiate by requesting that the seller fix things, and request additional inspections (i.e., mold inspector, structural engineer), and or a buyer's credit. This is an upfront cost for the buyer.

Appraisal Contingency: An appraisal is an unbiased estimate of what the true value of a home is worth. Buyers typically pay for the appraisal fee upfront, and the price varies. If the appraisal comes back less than the purchase price, the buyer can negotiate with the seller or cancel the transaction.

Mortgage Loan Options

Conventional Loan

-Insured by private lenders (i.e., bank, credit union, mortgage company)

-It is harder to get approved for these loans

-Sellers can pay 3-9% of buyer's closing cost

-Need at least a 620 credit score

-10yr, 15yr, or 30yr fixed rate mortgage repayment options

-Down payment can range 3-15% of purchase price

-Any down payment less than 20% requires Private Mortgage Insurance (PMI)

-Buyers can ask to have the PMI removed when the loan balance is paid down to 80% LTV (*loan-to-value*)

-PMI must be removed at 78% LTV

-Student Loans: The lender uses the payment listed on the credit report for each student loan when calculating debt (DTI). If the payment reflects $0 as the monthly payment, the lender has different guidelines they must follow depending on if the loan is in forbearance or deferment, or in a repayment plan option (i.e., income driven repayment plan).

Federal Housing Administration (FHA) Loan

-Insured by Federal Housing Administration

-Chances of approval are easier for this loan type

-Don't need great credit (500 credit score is accepted with a 10% down payment)

-Requires 3.5% down payment with a minimal credit score of 580

-Can purchase a 1-4 unit property

-Must be buyer's primary residence

-Sellers can pay up to 6% of buyer's closing cost

-15yr or 30yr fixed rate mortgage repayment options

-Student Loans: The lender uses the payment listed on the credit report for each student loan, or .5% of the loan balance when there is no payment requirement, when calculating the buyers' debt (DTI).

Department of Veteran Affairs (VA) Loan

-Backed by Department of Veteran's Affairs

-Government Loan

-Loan is for U.S. Veterans, active-duty service members, and widowed military spouses

-Issued by private lenders (i.e., banks, credit union, mortgage company)

-Zero percent down payment

-Sellers can pay up to 4% of buyer's closing cost

-No limit on the loan amount you can borrow

-Avoid paying Private Mortgage Insurance (PMI)

-No minimum credit score (best to still have at least a 620 or higher credit score)

-Can be used to buy, build, or refinance primary residence

-No prepayment penalties

-If buyer defaults on the loan, the VA will repay a portion of the loan back to lender

-VA can aid if buyer is facing foreclosure

Closing Disclosure

A **Closing Disclosure** is a form received before the closing, that provides final details about the mortgage loan the buyer has selected.

❑   Must receive **3 days** before closing

- ❏ Provides final details of mortgage loan
- ❏ Let's buyer know how much money they will need to bring to closing
- ❏ Shows a breakdown of fees and terms
- ❏ Shows projected monthly mortgage payment

Your **Journey to Success** has begun! You have a **CLEAR TO CLOSE** or you are on your way to one! Remember to celebrate all your successes no matter how small or big you think they are. In addition, it is important to remember that sometimes we fail on our journey and that is okay. Failure is needed for success. Continue to keep Killin the journey!

Notes: _____

_____

_____

_____

_____

_____

_____

_____

_____

_____

_____

_____

_____

_____

_____

Thank You for Joining the Journey!
www.odomhomes.com

Snowball Method

Debt	#1	#2	#3	#4	#5
Balance					
Monthly Payment					
January					
February					
March					
April					
May					
June					
July					
August					
September					
October					
November					
December					

Monthly Budget Tracker

Income

Paycheck #1 $_____
Paycheck #2 $_____
Paycheck #3 $_____
Other Income $_____
Other Income $_____
Income Total: $

Savings

Amount Saved:

5% of pay

10% of pay

Other:

Total Savings: $

Overall Total: $_____
Total Income: $_____
-
Overall Total: $_____
= $

Monthly Expenses

_____ $
_____ $
_____ $
_____ $
_____ $
_____ $
_____ $
_____ $
_____ $
_____ $
_____ $
_____ $
_____ $
_____ $
_____ $
_____ $
_____ $
_____ $

Cash Envelopes

Gas $_____
Grocery $_____
Household $_____
Spending Money $_____
_____ $_____
_____ $_____

References

(2020, September 9). *Consumer Financial Protection Bureau*
    https://www.consumerfinance.gov/ask-cfpb/what-is-a-loan-estimate-en-1995/

(2017, September 12). *Consumer Financial Protection Bureau*
    https://www.consumerfinance.gov/ask-cfpb/what-is-a-closing-disclosure-en-1983/

(n.d.). *Consumer Financial Protection Bureau*
    https://www.consumerfinance.gov/owning-a-home/loan-options/fha-loans/

Cruz-Martinez, G. (2021) *What is Whole Life Insurance and How Does It Work?*
    https://money.com/whole-life-insurance-guide/#:~:text=See%20An%20Estimate-,How%20Does%20
    Whole%20Life%20Insurance%20Work%3F,benefit%20upon%20the%20insured's%20death.

Daugherty, G. (2022, February 27). *Generational Wealth*
    https://www.investopedia.com/generational-wealth-definition-5189580

Escalante Troesh, J. (2018, May). *Build a Budget in 15 Minutes.* Purposeful Finance
    https://www.purposefulfinance.org/home/articles/the-15-minute-basic-budget?gclid=CjwKCAjw4ayUBhA4E
    iwATWyBrqS0kaLBEzAxyh5k5LnV5exHysxDFM05DBwnW_HfRRhXgpVMJ9ugShoCO7gQAvD_BwE

(n.d.). *Federal Trade Commission*
    https://www.ftc.gov/

(1997-2022). *FHA.com*
    https://www.fha.com/define/fha-loan

Fontinelle, A. (2021, May 9) *Importance of Home Inspection Contingency.*
    https://www.investopedia.com/articles/mortgages-real-estate/08/home-inspection.asp#:~:text=Home%20
    inspections%20can%20uncover%20potentially,step%20in%20purchasing%20a%20home.

Kurt, D. (2022). *Term vs. Whole Life Insurance: What's the Difference?*
    https://www.investopedia.com/term-life-vs-whole-life-5075430

Luthi, B. (2019, September 9). *What is a Conventional Loan.*
    https://www.experian.com/blogs/ask-experian/what-is-a-conventional-loan/#:~:text=A%20conventional%20
    loan%20is%20a,common%20type%20of%20mortgage%20loan.

Ramsey, D. (n.d.). *The Seven Baby Steps Dave Ramsey*
    https://www.ramseysolutions.com/dave-ramsey-7-baby-steps

Ramsey, D. (2022, April 13) *How the Debt Snowball Method Works*
    https://www.ramseysolutions.com/debt/how-the-debt-snowball-method-works

Strain, N. (2022, January 25) *Can I Use my 401 (K) to Buy a House*
    https://www.investopedia.com/ask/answers/081815/can-i-take-my-401k-buy-house.asp

Thoma, S. (n.d.) *The Four Uses of Cash*
    https://www.edwardjones.com/sites/default/files/acquiadam/2021-02/IPC-8343-A.pdf

Treece, D. (2022) *What is an Appraisal Contingency*
    https://www.forbes.com/advisor/mortgages/what-is-an-appraisal-contingency/

(n.d.). *U. S. Department of Urban Housing Development*
    https://www.hud.gov/buying/loans

(n.d.). *U.S. Department of Veteran Affairs*
    https://www.benefits.va.gov/homeloans/

(2022). *What Affects a Credit Scores.*
    https://www.experian.com/blogs/ask-experian/credit-education/score-basics/what-affects-your-credit-scores/

Printed in the United States
by Baker & Taylor Publisher Services